Every year nearly eight million
cats and dogs enter animal shelters in the U.S.

Three to four million are euthanized
because no home can be found for them.

This book is dedicated to the men and women
who run the shelters, and who work tirelessly
to find loving homes for the many
animals that come their way.

Published by: Sweet Memories Publishing
Sweet Memories, Inc.
Arnolds Park, IA

ISBN: 978-0-9762718-1-9

Library of Congress Control Number: 2007942556

Copyright © 2008 Jean Tennant

All rights reserved. No part of this book may be reproduced or transmitted in any form or by any means, electronic or mechanical, including photocopying, recording, or by an information storage and retrieval system, without permission in writing from the author.

First Printing April 2008

Outline Illustrations by Lauren Naig

Olivia's Birthday Puppy

By Jean Tennant

Outline illustrations by Lauren Naig

Graphic design by
Dedicated Business Solutions, Inc.
New Market, Iowa

It was Olivia's birthday, and her family gave her a party.

Her best friend Rae was there, and so was her Aunt Clarissa.

Everyone ate cake and ice cream. When they were finished, Olivia opened her presents. Her parents gave her a portable CD player. Rae gave her a scrapbook with pictures of them together in it.

When she opened her gift from her Aunt Clarissa, Olivia found a funny-looking bowl with two sides to it.

"What is it?" she asked.

"You've been asking for a puppy," her Aunt Clarissa explained. "Your mom and dad told me you're old enough now for a pet. That's my present to you."

Olivia was excited. "I'm getting a birthday puppy? Where is it?"

"A pet is a big responsibility," her aunt said. "Your puppy will become a member of your family and will be with you for many years. I want you to choose the right one."

"Today?" asked Olivia.

"No, not today," said Clarissa. "Today is your party. We'll go tomorrow."

That night Olivia hardly slept, thinking about her birthday puppy.

The next day Clarissa came to the house. First, they went by a pet store. They looked in the window and saw a pen full of chubby puppies.

"I'm going to tell you something important," Clarissa said. "You'll get to choose a pet, but I want you to think about it first. Puppies are wonderful little creatures, but there are many, many dogs that need homes. They're in shelters, just waiting for someone to adopt them and give them their 'forever' home."

A spotted puppy pressed his nose close to the window, and Olivia giggled.

"These puppies sure are cute," she said.

"Yes, they are," Clarissa agreed. "But I'd like to take you somewhere else to look for a pet."

Olivia agreed, and she waved good-bye to the puppies in the window as they walked away.

They got in Clarissa's car and drove to a building on the other side of town. The sign out front said RESCUE SHELTER.

"Remember my little dog, Freddie?" Clarissa asked. "I adopted him from a shelter when he was young. I loved him very much. I had him for a long time, until he was very old. I was sad when he died a couple of years ago."

"I remember Freddie," said Olivia. "I used to throw his favorite ball to him, and he'd bring it back to me."

They went inside the building. The veterinarian, Dr. Joe, was at the front desk.

"The Rescue Shelter takes in puppies and dogs that have been rescued from puppy mills or other terrible places," Clarissa explained to Olivia. "Or have been abandoned, or turned over by people who can't keep them any longer. Some are puppies, but most are adult dogs."

"When you adopt a rescue animal," Dr. Joe said, "you pay an adoption fee that's much less than what you'd pay at a pet store. The adoption fee is so all the pets here can have a thorough checkup and get their shots to keep them healthy."

"When you adopt an animal from a rescue shelter, you're giving a good home to an animal that needs a home," said Clarissa. "We're going to meet some dogs that are in foster care. That means they're staying in homes near here, just waiting for someone to love them and to adopt them."

At the first foster home they stopped at, there were five cute little dogs. Three of them ran up to greet Olivia.

"That's Bing, Kody and Topaz," the woman who lived there said.

One of the dogs happily approached Olivia.

"That's Topaz," the woman said. "She's three years old. She was rescued from a kennel where the dogs were very sad and neglected. She's house-trained now and has learned her manners. Topaz is ready to give some family a lot of love."

Kody and Bing jumped up until Olivia patted them, then they trotted off to play with their toys.

But Topaz climbed onto Olivia's lap and put her little face very close to Olivia's. When Olivia stroked her head, Topaz nudged Olivia's hand with her nose.

Olivia and Clarissa thanked the woman. As they left, Olivia looked back at the dogs. Topaz wanted to follow them out the door.

At the next foster home they went to, two dogs greeted them, tails wagging.

"That's Nika and Jackson," the people who lived there told Clarissa and Olivia. "Jackson is nine years old. His owner loved him and took good care of him, but when he went to live in a nursing home he couldn't take his pet with him. He made sure Jackson came to us so we would find him a good home."

"He's a nice little guy," said Clarissa to Olivia. "But you should probably have a younger dog."

Olivia stroked the dogs. She liked them both. But they weren't puppies, and she had wanted a puppy for her birthday.

When they left the second house, Olivia was yawning.

"Why are we looking at so many dogs?" she asked.

"Remember a couple of years ago, when your mom and dad bought a new house?" Clarissa asked her. "They looked at a lot of houses until they found the one that was just right for them. I want to be sure you get the pet that's the right one for you. Because when you choose a pet, it will be with you for the rest of its life. It has to be the right decision for both of you."

Olivia was disappointed.

"I didn't get my puppy today. When will I get one?"

"We'll look some more tomorrow," Clarissa promised.

That night Olivia dreamed about all the dogs they'd seen that day.

One dog especially stayed in her thoughts – one with big black eyes that had looked right at her and made her smile.

In the morning, Olivia looked at her birthday presents. There was no puppy there, but she opened the scrapbook her best friend Rae had given her. It had pictures of them together in it, from when Rae had moved in next door after being adopted by the family there.

Rae had talked to Olivia many times about being adopted. She loved her new parents and was happy they'd made her a part of their family.

After breakfast, Clarissa came to the house.

"We'll keep looking for your birthday puppy," she told Olivia.

But Olivia had already decided.

"I don't need a puppy," she said. "I like one of the dogs we met yesterday. I want to give Topaz her forever home."

"Topaz is a good choice for you," Clarissa agreed.

They went back to the house they'd been at the day before. The little dog, Topaz, ran to greet Olivia as soon as they walked in the door.

Topaz jumped into Olivia's arms.

"And I've decided I'm going to adopt Jackson," Clarissa said. "I like that he's an older dog. He's more settled, and that's what I want."

They filled out the adoption forms.

When they returned to Olivia's house later, they each had a new pet. Clarissa had Jackson, and Olivia had Topaz.

That night Topaz hopped onto Olivia's bed and curled up close to her with a contented sigh. Topaz had a loving family to care for her. She had her forever home.

And Olivia at last had her birthday present. As Topaz snuggled close, Olivia knew she'd made a good decision.

Printed in the United States
123655LV00002BA